Great
Napkin Folding
& Table Setting

Marianne Müller & Ola Mikolasek

with Hans Tapper

Sterling Publishing Co., Inc. New York

Translated by Elisabeth R. Reinersmann
English translation edited by Keith L. Schiffman

Library of Congress Cataloging-in-Publication Data

Müller, Marianne, Dipl.-Handelslehrerin.
    [Servietten falten. English]
    Great napkin folding & table setting / by Marianne Müller and Ota
Mikolasek with Hans Tapper ; [translated by Elisabeth R.
Reinersmann].
        p.   cm.
    Translation of: Servietten falten; and of: Der perfekt gedeckte
Tisch.
    Includes index.
    1. Napkin folding.   2. Table setting and decoration.
I. Mikolasek, Ota.   II. Tapper, Hans.   III. Müller, Marianne, Dipl.
-Handelslehrerin. Perfekt gedeckte Tisch. English. 1990.
    IV. Title.   V. Title: Great napkin folding and table setting.
TX879.M85   1990
642′.7—dc20   90-36204
                                                                CIP

10   9   8

English translation © 1990 by Sterling Publishing Co., Inc.
387 Park Avenue South, New York, N.Y. 10016
Original editions published in the Federal Republic of Germany
under the titles "Servietten falten: 80 Ideen für schön
gedeckte Tische" and "Der perfekt gedeckte Tisch"
© 1989 by Falken-Verlag GmbH, Niedernhausen/Ts.
Distributed in Canada by Sterling Publishing
% Canadian Manda Group, P.O. Box 920, Station U
Toronto, Ontario, Canada M8Z 5P9
Distributed in Great Britain and Europe by Cassell PLC
Villiers House, 41/47 Strand, London WC2N 5JE, England
Distributed in Australia by Capricorn Ltd.
P.O. Box 665, Lane Cove, NSW 2066
Printed and bound in Hong Kong
All rights reserved
Sterling ISBN 0-8069-7384-6 Paper

Thanks to the following manufacturers for supplying the items in this book: Schott-Zwiesel-Glaswerke AG (glasses), Villeroy & Boch AG (porcelain), M. H. Wilkens & Sohne GmbH (silverware), Carl Zollner KG (table linen). Thanks also to Deutsche Duni GmbH; Uti Stephan, Exclusiv Schenken und Wohnen. Thanks for the various themes for the table settings go to: Heike Backes, Petra Fey, Anke Heim, Siegfried Herrmann, Alice Keppel, Thomas Klemmer, Claudia Körkel, Tausseg Naz, Barbara Schmidt and Jürgen Wegmann.

Photos: Fotostudio Erbelding, Fotostudio Eichler + Hofmann, Rudi Scharf Fotostudios, Carl Zollner KG. Styling: Cornelia Adam. Drawings: Ulrike Hoffmann.

Contents

Introduction

Good company, good food, and fine wine are the important ingredients of a good meal. A beautifully set table, complete with the finest china, silverware, and glassware can turn that fine meal into an elegant event. Now you can set a table that's as elegant as any you've admired in a grand hotel, or in a five-star restaurant.

This book covers the preparation involved in setting a beautiful table, as well as the art of napkin folding. All of the steps necessary to dress a table are here—the proper way to spread a tablecloth, the placement of the silverware and the glassware, and the correct utensils to use with various menus. Not only will you learn how to set a beautiful table, but you will also learn why we use certain implements, and when and how they found their way to our tables. You will find brief historical notes about some common tableware in the following chapters.

Most of this book is dedicated to the art of napkin folding. The use of cloth napkins became

widespread early in the 19th century. Towards the end of the 19th century, napkin folding became a popular art form. Today, there is a renewed interest in the practice of formal table setting, and along with this renewed interest comes a renaissance of the art of napkin folding.

The eighty different napkin folds presented here are grouped according to their common basic folding steps. Step-by-step instructions will guide you through the folding process. The beginning, basic steps are always

precisely explained at the outset. A small drawing of this basic step is displayed at the top of each page.

The ten table settings shown at the end of this book should spark your imagination. Any of the ten could be adapted to other occasions, or modified to suit your personal tableware.

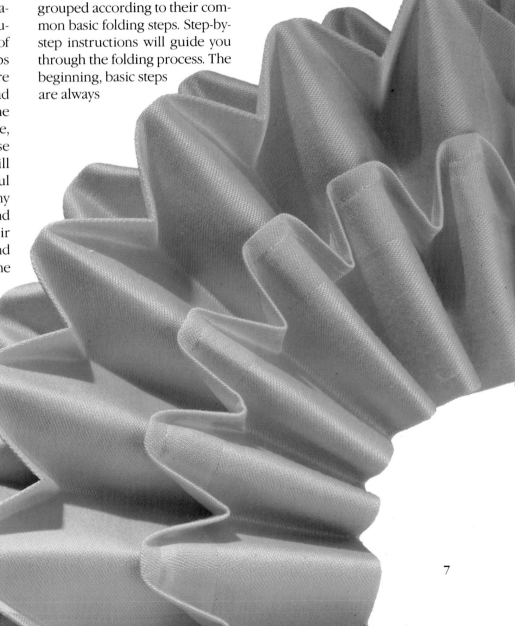

7

Glassware

The quality of good stemware can be judged by four criteria.

Surface strength is important for scratch and impact resistance. This surface strength gives glass its chime-like sound.

In order for the wine to show its unadulterated color, the glass must be free of any "sediment" and must be of a neutral color by day and by night.

A glass should have a thin and even edge, for aesthetic reasons as well as for smooth contact with the lips.

These first three criteria give a glass a certain elasticity which adds to its strength and tolerance when raised for a toast, and when washed.

Finally, a glass must be well proportioned, with a low center of gravity to prevent easy spilling, even when filled.

In addition to these four criteria, it is important that when glasses are washed in the dishwasher, the washing will give the glass an optimal shine. Therefore, the glass must be resistant to temperature changes and to harsh chemicals.

The foot of the glass should be flat on the bottom so that no water residue can collect there and thus discolor the glass. The opening of the glass should be wide enough so that it can be easily washed and dried by hand.

Select from a stock that allows you to replace broken pieces, even after some time has passed.

A second set of stemware for special occasions is a must for an elegant life-style. Lead crystal stemware is a good choice. These glasses will make your table sparkle, and they also let your guests know how much they mean to you.

Choosing a proper wine glass for the wine being served is the mark of a competent host. The expert will know that a chilled white wine is served in a small glass, so that the wine does not lose its chill. Red wine needs volume to bring out its full bouquet, and it should be served in larger glasses. Rosé is best served in a goblet. When drinking from a glass with a fluted edge, *more* of the liquid flows with each swallow, allowing the full body and taste of the wine to unfold. This is true for red wines and for rosé.

A glass that curves in at the opening allows *less* liquid to reach the tongue with each swallow. This allows the fruity flavor of some wines to unfold.

Red wine needs to be exposed to air in order to unfold its special bouquet. A large glass with a wide opening fulfills this requirement. Exposing the wine to

Red wine glass   White wine glass   Dessert wine glass   Sherry glass

Champagne "tulip"   Champagne flute   Champagne "coupe"

oxygen can be augmented by swirling the wine in the glass in careful, slow circular movements.

The trend towards larger wine glasses has changed the way wine is poured. Not too long ago, it was customary to fill a glass two-thirds. Today, the larger glasses are only filled halfway, or only up to the widest point of the bowl. This expanded surface allows the wine to unfold its full bouquet.

Champagne occupies a very special place as the drink of choice for very special occa-sions—the birth of a child, wed-dings, and formal dinners. Once champagne was used only for a special toast—now it is often the wine for a whole evening. The glass used to serve champagne should enhance this very special "bubbly." Greet your guests with champagne to guarantee a stimu-lating party. It's just as wonderful to end an evening with a glass of champagne.

Let's remember the *aperitif* that always gets the party going. One of the classics is the ever-popular sherry. The many vari-eties of this favorite—from very dry to pleasantly sweet—make it a must for any occasion. The glass used to serve sherry en-hances its character. The tem-perature of the sherry is impor-tant—some, like the Fino and Manzanilla, should be well chilled. A small tulip-shaped goblet (like the "copita") is a good choice for sherry.

Clearly, the glass plays a very important role, even when no more than juice or mineral water is served.

Silverware

The fork, the youngest member of the silverware family, originated in the Orient. It has been on our dinner table only for the last few centuries. The knife's history dates back to the Stone Age, when it was used for hunting as well as for eating. Liquids were drunk by hunters and gatherers who used hollow-shaped natural products, such as shells. The first man-made spoons were made from wood, bone or horn. Wood was, for the longest time, the material of choice.

Knife and spoon were considered personal property and were carried by each diner in a special pouch that was attached to the belt. To eat solid food, people used their fingers or the tip of the knife. During the Middle Ages—in the monasteries— eating habits began to change for the better.

In the Renaissance, people began to rediscover some of the pleasures of life, influenced largely by contact with the Orient. Eating was elevated to new heights. People who knew how to cook were in demand. Carving (done with fork and knife) became an art form, and eating utensils were decorated.

Silverware also changed: it became lighter, knife tips became more rounded (the fork had taken over the job of piercing), and knife handles became longer. In later centuries people began to consider knife, fork, and spoon as a set and decorated them accordingly, manufacturing a dozen or more of them at a time. It became a custom to give a set of silverware to each guest. The introduction of coffee and tea encouraged social gatherings, which in turn resulted in new pieces of silverware: coffee, tea, and mocha spoons, sugar tongs and cookie tongs. Many of the special utensils that are still in use today came into being during the Renaissance, such as the cutlery used to serve fruit, dessert, and fish, oyster forks, special cutlery to eat caviar and shellfish, soup ladles, and punch bowl utensils.

It seems as if the history of silverware is also the history of our culture. Food is not only one of life's necessities, but it is also one of life's most pleasurable experiences.

From left to right: fruit fork, fruit knife, cake fork, compote spoon, coffee spoon, mocha spoon, gourmet spoon, oyster fork, lobster fork, caviar knife and caviar spoon.

From left to right (above): dessert fork, dessert knife, and dessert spoon, dinner fork and dinner knife, soupspoon (this large spoon is used when soup is served in soup plates; if soup is served in soup bowls or cups, a smaller, somewhat more rounded spoon or the dessert spoon is used), fish fork, and fish knife.

Porcelain

Porcelain belongs to the family of ceramics, which includes everything from bricks, faience, and stoneware, to the finest porcelain.

Recent information suggests that the Chinese (after much experimentation) were making porcelain as long ago as 1000 B.C. Not until the 13th century did a few pieces reach Europe, where it was literally exchanged, pound for pound, for gold. Marco Polo is said to have given it its name: "porcella," the Italian name for a porcelainlike seashell. It was not until the 17th century that porcelain reached Europe in great quantities. The making of porcelain, however, remained a well-kept secret in China.

Porcelain was reinvented in Germany in 1709. Augustus II had an experimental laboratory in Dresden where he tried to make gold. His alchemist/pharmacist Karl Friedrich Bottger discovered instead the secret of making porcelain. The experimental laboratory became a porcelain factory. The factory was later moved to Meissen. Porcelain manufacturing was later extended to cities such as Vienna, Chelsea, and Copenhagen, as well as to other cities in Germany.

To judge porcelain's quality, hold it up to the light to examine its translucency. Other criteria include surface brilliance, richness of tone, and clear color (from bluish white to warm ivory). Fragments should always break off straight and cracks should not absorb liquid.

Experts distinguish between "hard" porcelain (manufactured in Europe), and "soft" porcelain (from China, Japan, and England). Porcelain's popularity, nobility and its acknowledged preciousness remain unabated over the centuries.

Porcelain manufacturers have established a special branch solely to accommodate the needs of the hotel industry. This industry (including the closely related restaurant industry) makes great demands on the porcelain manufacturers. The porcelain for use in hotel and restaurants must have good, smooth surface glaze that must be resistant to chemicals, and it must withstand the constant stress of mechanical handling. It must have exceptional surface strength to resist chipping, scratching, and cutting. It must be neutral in both color and odor.

In addition to these requirements, porcelain for the hotel and restaurant industry must have a certain thickness, and it must be resistant to breakage. It must also be easy to stack plates, bowls, and cups. The manufacturer must have on hand an ample stock of any pattern.

The hotel and catering business must have (in addition to the everyday dinnerware) the necessary inventory to accommodate requests for formal and festive occasions that require special table settings and special, festive dinnerware, silverware, and stemware.

Special effects can be achieved with "place plates." These can be made either from porcelain, glass, or metal. Place plates in contrasting colors or with silver or gold borders make for a very special table decor.

Porcelain place plate.

Glass place plate.

Metal place plate.

Bottom: mocha cup and saucer.
Middle left: coffee cup and saucer.
Middle right: soup cup/bowl on a saucer.
Top left: dessert/breakfast plate.
Top right, from top to bottom: salad plate, hors d'oeuvre plate, and two dinner plates.

Preparation

Setting a table must begin with good preparation and organization. Seating order is usually the first step in setting a formal table. Check carefully for the perfect cleanliness of the dinnerware, silverware, and stemware that is to be used.

Get the room and table(s) ready. Choose the appropriate tablecloth as well as all the dinnerware, silverware, and stemware.

TABLECLOTH

During laundering and ironing, the tablecloth is given several vertical and horizontal creases. If more than one tablecloth is used, the direction of the creases should be carefully matched. Join the tablecloths at corresponding creases.

Unfold the tablecloth lengthwise and position it on the table at right angles in front of you, so that the open side with the middle crease faces you. Hold the cloth between your thumb and your index finger at the center crease while holding (at the same time) the top layer, and then spread out your arms, lifting the cloth slightly.

Allow the cloth to extend 8 to 10 inches below the edge of the opposite side of the table. Pull the cloth towards you. The cloth will now cover the table smoothly and it should be perfectly even. See the photos on the opposite page.

SETTING THE TABLE

Setting a table could include any arrangement from the simplest to the most formal. Strictly speaking, a "plain" table setting consists of only a knife, a fork, and a napkin. Each additional piece could be considered an elaboration of the setting.

Begin setting the table by placing the napkin, either folded or unfolded, or a place plate on a designated spot on the table. The silverware is then positioned on the table—fork on the left side, knife on the right side, with the knife edge facing the plate.

If any additional pieces of silverware are added, do so from the inside out. The guest (on the other hand) will use the silverware in the opposite order—from the outside in.

Place the bread plate with the butter knife (knife edge to the outside) on the left side of the fork. The soupspoon is placed to the right of the knife. If a fish dish is served between the soup and the entrée, place the fish fork to the outside of the dinner fork. Place the fish knife on the right side, parallel to the dinner knife. Place the soupspoon on the right and the outside, next to the fish knife.

Generally, there should be no more than three pieces of silverware on the left of the plate, and no more than four pieces of silverware on the right side of the plate.

The dessert silverware (fork and spoon), as well as the cheese knife, are placed at the head of the plate. The choice of silverware depends upon the menu. If an hors d'oeuvre is served, use the middle set pictured on page 10. For a fish dish, use the appropriate silverware pictured on the same page. If the hors d'oeuvre is served in a glass or in a small bowl, use the fork and a small spoon from the middle set shown on page 10.

POSITIONING THE STEMWARE

Position the stemware according to the sequence in which the different wines are to be served. The stemware is positioned after everything else, including the napkins, is in place.

Position the glass for the wine served with the main course directly above the tip of the knife. This glass is sometimes called the "guide" glass. If a drink is served prior to the meal, that glass will be positioned in front of the "guide" glass. The after-dinner drink will stand *behind* the "guide" glass. Position the glasses so that the guest will be able to reach each without having to maneuver around any of the other glasses at his place. Put no more than four glasses next to each setting. You may need some additional glasses. If two different white wine selections are offered, two different glasses are required. The guest should be able to enjoy each wine separately.

Spreading the tablecloth. Unfold the top half of the tablecloth, and spread it out, so that it overhangs the edge 8 to 10 inches on the side opposite you. The open side of the tablecloth with the center fold on top now faces you. Take the tablecloth with both hands, with the fold between the middle finger and the index finger of one hand, and at the same time, hold the top part of the tablecloth between the thumb and the index finger of the other hand.

Changing the tablecloth. If you want to change the tablecloth while your guests are still at the table: place the clean tablecloth as previously described, overhanging the opposite edge 8 to 10 inches; fold the used tablecloth underneath back to the side opposite you.

Pull both tablecloths towards you, so your guests won't see the soiled tablecloth. By combining these two steps, you'll avoid disturbing your guests.

With both arms spread, lift the tablecloth.

Take the new tablecloth with both hands, and at the same time, pick up the old tablecloth along with the new one.

The new tablecloth is now placed smoothly on the table.

1 When setting a table, designate each place using either the dinner plate, the place plate, or a napkin. The plate determines the position of the silverware that will be used for the main course.

2 If a place plate is used, it serves as the perfect place for the napkin.

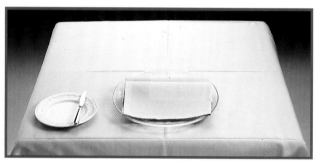

3 Place the bread/roll plate, with the butter knife (knife edge to the outside) on top of it, to the left of the place plate.

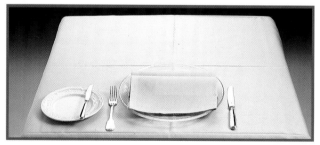

4 The different pieces of silverware are arranged from the inside out. The dinner knife is on the right side with the edge to the inside, the fork is on the left. Again, place the silverware in relation either to the place plate or to the dinner plate.

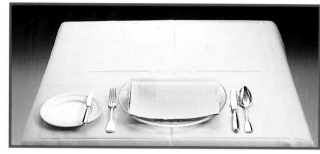

5 If soup is served, place the soupspoon to the outside of the dinner knife, on the right.

6 Place the silverware for dessert above the plate. The fork handle should point to the left, the spoon handle to the right.

7 Place the glass for the wine that accompanies the main course directly above the tip of the dinner knife, on the right.

8 This setting has been made for the following menu: a cold fish hors d'oeuvre, soup, a main course with meat, and cheese for dessert. The silverware for the cheese is above the plate; the knife handle points to the right; the cheese fork's handle points to the left. The glass for the white wine (for the fish course) is to the right and below the glass for the red wine (for the main course).

1 White wine glass, red wine glass, and champagne glass; butter knife; silverware for the hors d'oeuvre; soupspoon; silverware for the main course; the dessert fork, and the dessert spoon; the plate for bread or rolls. The place plate with a napkin is for a meal of a cold hors d'oeuvre with bread and butter and white wine, soup, and a main course served with red wine. The meal ends with cheese and champagne.

4 White wine glass, red wine glass, and champagne glass; butter knife; soupspoon; silverware for fish, the main course, and for dessert; a plate for bread/rolls; a place plate with a napkin. This setting is for a meal of a cold hors d'oeuvre with bread and butter and white wine, soup, a main course with red wine, and dessert with champagne.

5 White wine glass, burgundy glass, and champagne glass; butter knife; silverware for the main course and for dessert; a place plate with a napkin. This setting is for a meal of soup with bread/roll, a hot hors d'oeuvre with white wine, and a main course with burgundy and dessert with champagne.

2 White wine glass, red wine glass, and champagne glass; silverware for bread and butter, soup, fish, the main course and dessert. The place plate with a napkin is for a meal of soup with bread/rolls and butter, a hot fish dish with white wine, a main course with red wine, and a dessert with champagne.

3 Champagne glass, red wine glass, and rosé wine glass; butter knife; fish fork, and fish knife; soupspoon; dinner fork, dinner knife; cheese fork, and cheese knife; a plate for bread/rolls; a place plate with a napkin. This setting is for a meal of a cold fish hors d'oeuvre with bread and butter and champagne, soup, a main course with red wine, and cheese with rosé wine.

Napkins

Today we have a wide variety of napkin materials to choose from. Aside from traditional napkins made from fabric, there are also paper napkins. They all come in an assortment of sizes, colors and prints. Paper napkins are pre-folded, of course, and the creases in them can not be removed. For that reason, paper napkins are not always suitable for some of the projects. However, if a particular folding technique calls for those very creases, then paper napkins are ideal.

A formal table requires nothing less than a fabric napkin. Fabric napkins are available in a variety of materials. Acrylic blends make very soft, limp napkins. Felt

is sometimes used for table padding, and for stiffer, decorative table spreads. Manufacturers seldom use linen anymore, but prefer a blend instead. Many favor cotton. The standard sizes available in the United States are: 10″×10″, 13″×13″, 17″×17″, and 20″×20″. Standard sizes available in Europe include: 32×32 cm, 40×40 cm, 50×50 cm, and 60×60 cm. The 17″×17″ napkin will serve as a good substitute for either the 40×40 cm napkin or for the 50×50 cm napkin. Fabric napkins come in a variety of sizes: 10″×10″ (32×32 cm) napkins are for tea or breakfast napkins. These are suitable for uncomplicated projects only. The more complicated napkin folds require napkins measuring either 17″×17″ (40×40 cm) or 20″×20″ (60×60 cm). The most practical and commonly used size, one that allows you to reproduce all the samples in this book, measures 17″×17″ (40×40 cm or 50×50 cm) and is made of cotton. You could use rectangular napkins, but you would have to make one additional fold at the outset, so that you could work with a true square.

The type of weave of the fabric that you use will determine the ease or difficulty of folding a particular form. Most of the time linen or damask is used. While damask gives the material a flowing texture, it wears out rather quickly. Regardless of the texture of the material, starch the napkins before beginning your project. For some of the examples shown, only light starching is needed, for others heavier starching is a must. It requires a bit more work to fold a well-starched napkin.

To ensure that the results of your folding projects are as perfect as possible, here are two important tips. Reinforce all the folds as you go along to make sure the napkin will hold up. Store napkins flat and unfolded after they have been laundered. Creases in a napkin often interfere with folding.

Group A

This group has some basic steps that are used for many projects.

Although the napkin is folded in half each time, make sure that the open side is pointed in the proper direction. Subsequent folding steps depend on that position.

1　Position a square napkin flat on the table with the inside facing up.

4　Same as step 2, but fold the upper edge to the lower edge, with the open side pointing down.

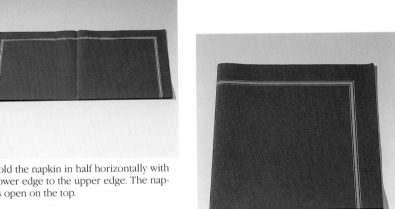

2　Fold the napkin in half horizontally with the lower edge to the upper edge. The napkin is open on the top.

3　Continue folding vertically either to the left or to the right, creating a square again.

5　Fold the napkin in half vertically with the open side pointing to the right.

1 Half-Roll
2 Double Roll
3 Roll

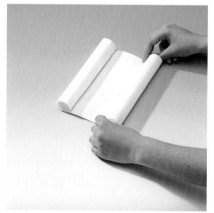

1 Fold the napkin in half horizontally, with the lower edge to the upper edge; roll the napkin from the left side to the middle.

2 Fold the napkin as above, and roll the right side of the napkin to the middle, forming a double roll.

3 Fold the napkin as in step 1, but continue rolling the napkin all the way to the end to form a roll.

If you use standard dinner plates, the best size for the napkin is 17″×17″. A larger napkin will also look good when place plates are used.

4 *Double Wave*
5 *Triple Wave*

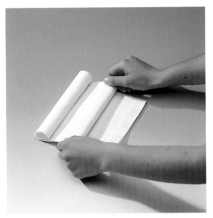

4a Fold a "half-roll," and turn the napkin over.

4b Now roll the right half to the middle.

5 Proceed as in 4a, and fold the remaining portion of the napkin into two folds.

The "half-roll" is the starting point for both the double wave (shown on the plate) and the triple wave (shown to the left of the plate). Napkin size: 17″×17″.

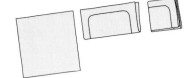

6 Single Pocket
7 Triple Pocket

Insert either a silk flower arrangement, some candy, or a dessert fork into the pocket to add to the beauty of the table setting.

If the table setting is exclusively for coffee and cake, use a 10″×10″ or 13″×13″ napkin.

6 Fold the napkin according to the basic step, creating a square, and then tuck the upper layer under and inside.

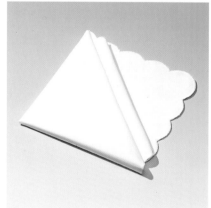

7a Fold as above and then tuck the next layer under and inside.

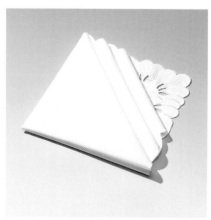

7b Now tuck the third layer under and inside to expose the corner design.

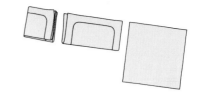

8   Pocket with One Cuff
9   Pocket with Two Cuffs

8   This is a variation of the "single pocket" napkin on the previous page. Fold the second layer to the outside.

9a   Follow the basic step, folding a square with the open sides to the right and facing up. Fold the top layer to the outside.

9b   Fold the napkin as in 9a and then fold the second layer partially to the outside to show the corner design.

For this type of folding technique you might want to use paper napkins since they are already folded into the proper form, and already have the necessary creases.

Example 9b will hide the not-so-pretty "wrong" side of the napkin which is shown exposed in example 9a. Position such a napkin on the table with the right side up, and with the design in the lower right corner.

10 *Simple Cap*
11 *Maid's Cap*

10a   First fold the napkin into a square and then fold on the diagonal, so the tips are pointing up.

10b   Fold both the left and the right corners into each other.

11a   Pull down the tips of the "simple cap" as shown.

11b   A variation with a different-color inlay: slide triangles of a contrasting-color paper between the napkin layers.

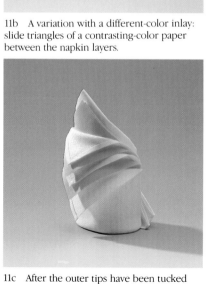

11c   After the outer tips have been tucked into each other, pull the top tips down.

The colored paper used for the inlays should be coordinated with the color of the table setting. See an example on page 88 for the Japanese theme.

12   Cap with Cuff
13   Cap with Turned-Down Cuff

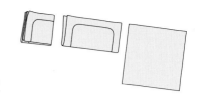

12a   Fold napkin according to basic steps. Fold the napkin into a square, then a triangle. Lower portion partially covers upper.

12b   Tuck both outer tips into each other.

13   To create the "cap with turned-down cuff," fold the top corner down.

The "cap with turned-down cuff" (on the plate) is a variation of the "cap with cuff" (left). Insert a silk flower into the pocket for a new twist.

14 Tricorn
15 Melon

14a   Fold the napkin first into a square according to the basic step, and then into a triangle.

14b   Fold the upper portion down over the lower edge.

Begin the basic step with the right side of the napkin up and fold it into a square from the left to the right. In case the rolled left lower corner does not stay firmly in place, skip this step and just roll the first layer across to the middle.

15a   From a square, tightly roll the layers to the middle.

15b   When finished, the napkin should look like the photo.

15c   Roll the lower corner to the middle.

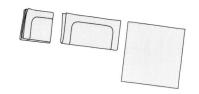

16 *Butterfly*
17 *Blossom*

16a   Fold the upper corner diagonally to the lower corner.

16b   Fold this corner twice to the middle.

16c   Do the same with the next top layer of the upper corner.

16d   Fold the napkin diagonally back.

If the "wrong" side of the napkin is not very pretty (perhaps the stitching of the lace is showing), start the basic folding steps for the butterfly and for the blossom with the "right" side of the napkin facing you.

17   Fold both the left and the right corners into each other.

29

18 Cone
19 Hat

18a Fold both of the upper right layers diagonally and tuck them under and then inside.

18b Slide your hand into the pocket, turning the cone halfway to the right.

19 Flatten the cone, turn the napkin, and then fold the lower tip up.

Both of these folding ideas lend themselves well to 17″×17″ napkins. If the napkins are well starched, the hat will stay upright on the table. The cone (if not flattened out) will hold the silverware.

20 Bishop's Mitre

20a Fold napkin horizontally, lower edge to upper edge. Fold upper left and lower right corners diagonally to the middle.

20b Turn the napkin over so that the upper right corner is now on the lower left side.

20c Fold the napkin in the middle and lift up the hidden triangle.

20d Fold the right side to the left side and underneath the triangle.

20e Fold back the left side and tuck it into the triangle.

The "bishop's mitre" is particularly striking when the napkin has contrasting stripes or borders.

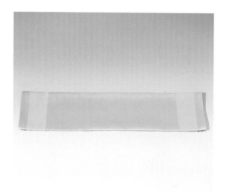

21a Fold the napkin in half, as shown.

21b Fold both sides to the middle, duplicating the form shown.

21c Turn the napkin over and roll both extensions into cones.

21d Fold together at the middle and stand the napkin upright.

22 Fold as described for the megaphone, but don't turn it over as in 21c.

Napkins for both forms need to be well starched. The cones should be rolled up tightly. If you use paper napkins, flatten the cones so that they won't come undone easily.

23   *Star-Shaped Fan*

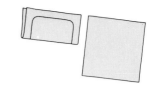

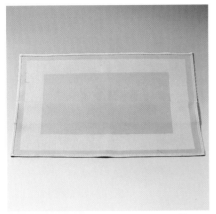

23a   Start with the napkin folded in half, with the open side pointing up. Fold down approximately two-thirds of the upper layer.

23b   Turn the napkin over and fold down two-thirds.

23c   Fold up the lower edge one-third on both sides.

You will not notice the seam of the napkin as much if you do the first step (folding the napkin in half) with the "wrong" side of the material facing you.

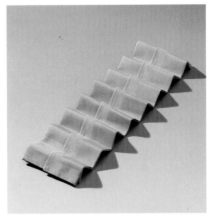

23d   Fold the napkin in six to eight even folds.

23e   Pull each deep fold forward.

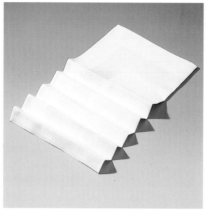

24 Upright Fan
25 Simple Fan

24a   Fold the napkin (folded in half) into ¾"-deep folds, slightly beyond the middle.

24b   Fold the napkin in half, as shown.

24c   Fold the right rectangular portion to the left, towards the fan.

It isn't important if the open end of the folded napkin points up or down. Just make sure the napkin is well starched.

24d   Turn down the extended portion and stand the napkin upright.

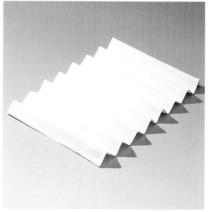

25   For the "simple fan," pleat the whole napkin.

26a Fold the napkin in half, with the open side pointing down. Fold up two-thirds of the upper layer past the middle crease.

26b Turn the napkin over and repeat on the other side.

All the fanlike forms look best if the folds are as symmetrical as possible. The only requirement is that the napkins be well starched.

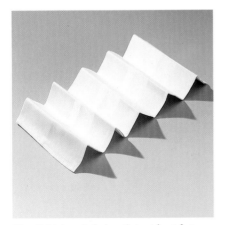

26c Fold the whole length in at least five equal folds.

26d Hold the napkin in one hand at the open side and pull out each deep fold.

26e Do likewise at the other side and then press folds firmly together.

27a Fold the napkin in half; then pull down the upper left and the right corners without creasing the material.

27b Fold both sides together and stand the napkin upright.

This is an easy but very effective form to fold. It can be made from any size napkin—a large one for a dinner setting or a small one for a breakfast setting.

28a Fold only the upper left corner down. Do not crease the fabric.

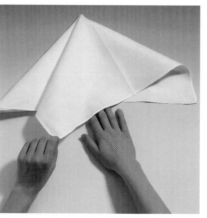

28b Fold the lower right corner of the upper layer over to the left.

28c Fold a right triangle to the left and stand the napkin upright.

29 Fancy Tent

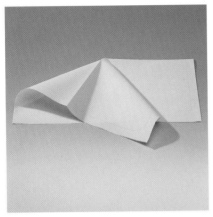

29a Fold the napkin in half, open side pointing down. Fold lower left corner of the upper layer to the right to form a triangle.

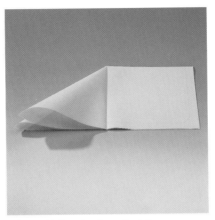

29b Fold the triangle to the left.

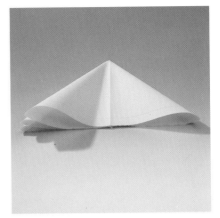

29c Fold the right corner (as in 29a) to form a triangle.

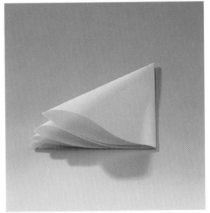

29d Fold the triangle to the left.

The "fancy tent" can be made using a paper napkin; the existing creases are the same as those needed to fold the "fancy tent."

29e Pick up the napkin without creasing the folds.

30   Triple Fan
31   Pointed Triple Fan

30a   Fold the napkin in half with the open side pointing down. Fold up the upper layer a little less than half.

31   Pull out the bottom folds of the triple fan.

30b   Fold up the lower portion so that you have three layers of equal size.

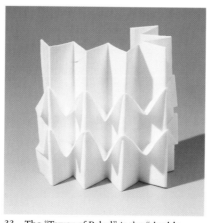

32   To make the "double-pointed triple fan," pull out the middle folds as well.

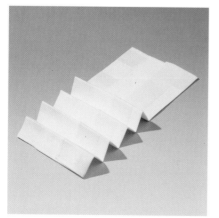

30c   Fold the napkin in six or eight equal folds, and then form a fan.

33   The "Tower of Babel" is the "double-pointed triple fan" joined together, creating a tower.

These napkins are easy to duplicate, despite the cumbersome procedure of pulling down the tips. Even that is not too difficult, if you hold the napkin firmly together on one end.

34 Arrow

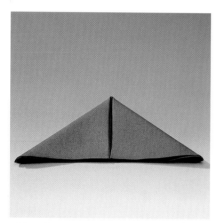

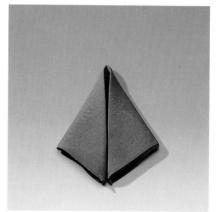

34a Fold the napkin in half, with the open side pointing down; then fold both upper corners down to the middle.

34b Continue folding the outer corners down to the middle to form a point.

34c Turn the napkin over and fold the center tips back for the "feet"; then stand the napkin upright.

Both sides of the arrow create a triangle. The "feet" are in the back. Since this design looks rather sober, consider some additional decoration.

35 Chinese Junk

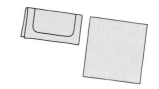

35a Fold the napkin in half, with the open side pointing down; then fold the right half over to the left to form a square.

35b Fold the open (lower left) corners to the upper right corner; then turn the napkin as shown, creating a triangle.

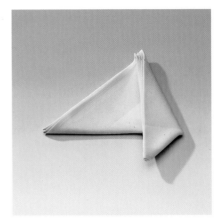

35c Fold both lower corners to the middle to form a tip.

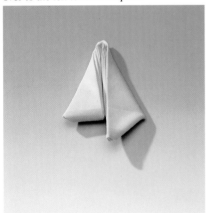

35d Turn both lower tips under and towards the back, and then reinforce the crease.

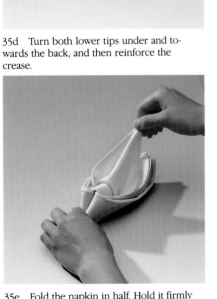

35e Fold the napkin in half. Hold it firmly at the blunt side and then pull out each individual layer.

The Chinese junk is not quite as difficult to create as it might seem. Make sure that you hold on firmly to the blunt edge when you "hoist the sails."

36a Fold the napkin in half with the open side pointing to the right; then fold both upper corners to the middle.

36b Fold the triangle down.

36c Turn the napkin over and fold both upper corners down again.

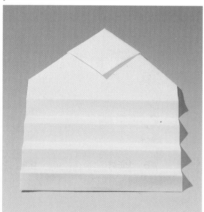

36d Turn the napkin over again and fold the lower portion into folds.

36e Hold the napkin securely under the tip of the square. Unfold on both sides.

A feltlike material was used for this "fancy fan." The last fold is smaller than the rest, making the transition to the flat portion of the napkin more interesting.

37 *Cardinal's Hat*

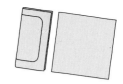

37a   Fold napkin in half, open side pointing to the left; then fold upper edge twice to the back, and lower edge twice to the front.

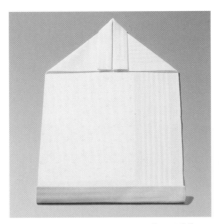

37b   Fold the upper corners to the middle, showing the cuff.

37c   Fold the lower portion up to the top as shown, and then fold both the left and the right corners down.

The napkin for the "cardinal's hat" must be at least 20″ × 20″, since it would be difficult to tuck both ends together because of the numerous folds required.

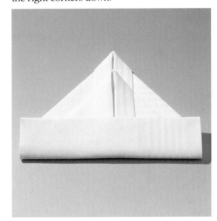

37d   Fold the lower portion up to create the form shown.

37e   Tuck the left side into the right side.

Group B

Fold the forms belonging to Group B using the following basic steps. The basic steps necessary for each individual napkin fold are shown in diagrams in the upper corner of each following page.

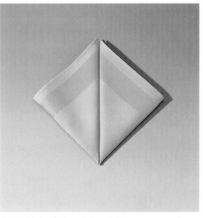

3   Fold the left and the right corners up to the middle. Hold the napkin securely in place with your thumbnail at the middle, while folding the corners up.

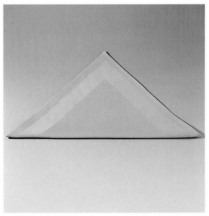

2   Create a triangle by folding the lower corner up to the upper corner.

1   Position the napkin diagonally in front of you, with the left ("wrong") side facing up.

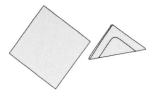

38 Envelope

38a After following the basic steps, fold both lower corners to the middle.

38b Continue folding the outer portions to the middle.

38c The napkin should look like this after doing the two preceding steps.

This envelope has been folded from a 20″ × 20″ napkin. You could use a 17″ × 17″ paper napkin.

38d Fold the lower portion of the napkin up to the base of the triangle.

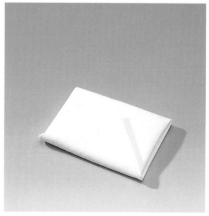

38e Fold the triangle down to give you the envelope shape.

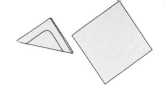

39 Dinner Jacket
40 Tuxedo

39a Fold the napkin according to the basic steps; then fold the lower edge up approximately 1″.

39b Turn the napkin over and then fold both upper corners down to the middle.

39c Fold both sides back to create the napkin shape shown.

39d Finish the jacket by folding the lower portion back; then decorate the jacket with a ribbon.

40 Create a shawl as shown by folding the lower edge first. Continue as directed for the dinner jacket from step 39b.

The bow tie adds that final touch to the dinner jacket or to the tuxedo. Use laminated ribbon or lace and just lay it on top of the napkin.

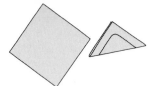

41 *Bird's Wing*
42 *Palm Frond*
43 *Scallop*

41a Fold the triangle accordion-style. The upper tip is on the bottom.

41b Fold the napkin together in the middle and set it on the table on its side.

42 For the palm frond, pin together both tips at the top, and then set the napkin upright.

43 Form the scallop by giving the "palm frond" a wider base, as shown on the opposite page.

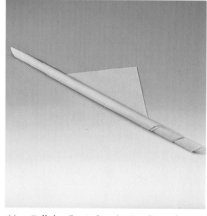

44a Roll the (basic form) triangle up from the lower edge, leaving the upper corner exposed.

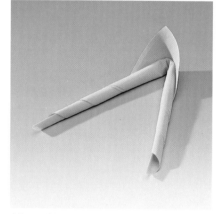

44b Fold the napkin in the middle; stand the napkin upright to give it a base for support.

45 Continue rolling the (basic form) triangle to the top. Fold it and set it into a glass.

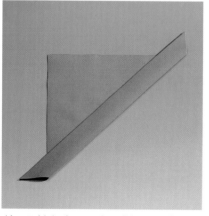

46a Fold the lower edge of the triangle up (approximately 1″).

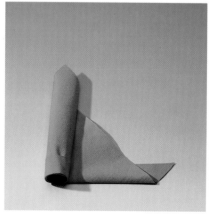

46b Turn the napkin over and roll it up, tucking the end into the pocket.

44 Divining Rod
45 Cigar
46 Column

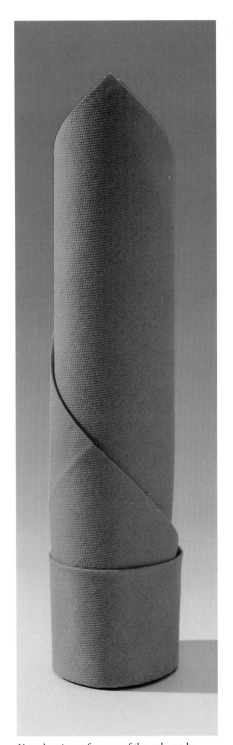

A 17″ × 17″ napkin is sufficient for these forms. The "palm frond" can be easily folded, secured with a pin at the top, and then set upright. Use a well-starched fabric napkin.

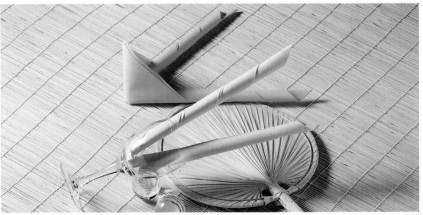

Vary the circumference of the column by changing the tightness of the roll.

These examples are also best when made from a 17″ × 17″ napkin. The "cigar" can be tied together and placed next to the plate, instead of putting it into a glass.

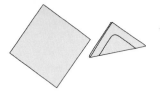

47 Obelisk

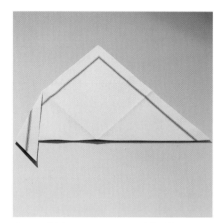

47a Fold down one corner of the (basic form) triangle.

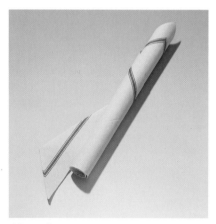

47b Roll up the napkin along the lower edge from the opposite side.

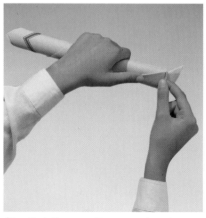

47c Tuck the extending corner into the opening at the bottom.

The larger the napkin, the taller the obelisk. A 10″ × 10″ or 17″ × 17″ paper napkin would be best for this project.

48 Candle

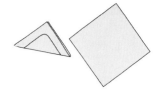

48a   Fold the upper corner down to the lower edge.

48b   Fold back the upper layer of the tip so that it extends slightly above the top edge.

48c   Twist that tip to form the flame of the candle.

Set the "candle" into a glass, or tie a ribbon around it. If fabric is used, and the table surface is not too smooth, the folded napkin will hold together well without additional support.

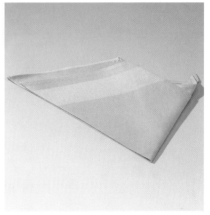

48d   Fold the right portion over to the left, in front of the "flame."

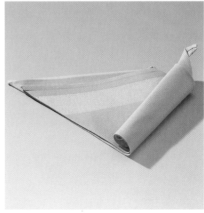

48e   Roll the napkin from the right to the left.

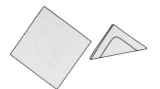

49 *Cowboy Hat*

49a Fold both lower corners as shown, making sure that the seams are parallel to the lower edge.

49b Fold down the upper layer of the top portion.

49c Turn the napkin over and fold down the upper corner.

To hide the seams, position the napkin with the "right" side facing up, when starting the first basic step. Form the hat into an oval shape, and then push the upper portion slightly to the inside.

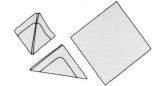

50 *Pansy*

50a   Complete the first three basic steps, and then fold the square in half.

50b   Fold the lower edge into three folds, and then turn the napkin.

50c   Pull down all three tips, and then turn the corners slightly back.

The pansy is a wonderful addition to an intimate table setting. A small napkin with delicate lace is ideal. Your creation will be just as attractive if displayed in a wine glass.

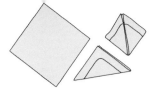

51 Bishop's Hat

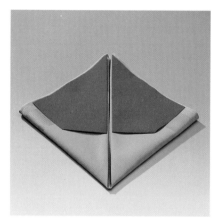

51a Fold according to the diagram above; cut paper napkins of a contrasting color and place them as shown.

51b Fold the lower portion in the middle to create a triangle.

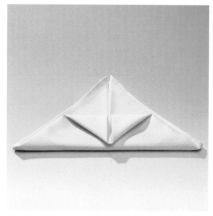

51c Fold the tip of the upper layer back to the lower edge.

Here are both versions. The two-colored finished version in the photo on page 88 is an example of the effect that can be created with such a design.

51d Tuck the left and the right corners into each other in the back; pull down both upper tips, tucking them into the cuffs.

51e This is an example using two colors.

52 Banana
53 Corn on the Cob

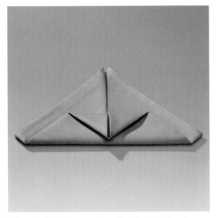

52a Follow instructions for the "bishop's hat," but don't fold the lower half of the form all the way up to the tip.

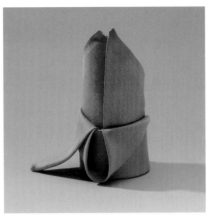

52b Pull down both tips as if you were peeling a banana.

53 For the "corn on the cob," peel the top layer of the center point down.

The napkin on the dinner plate looks like a half-peeled banana. Pull down the top layer to show the "silk threads" of "corn on the cob."

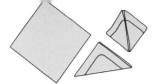

54 *Spire*
55 *Double Door*
56 *Arch*

54a   After completing the three basic steps, fold the lower half of the napkin up and back.

54b   Turn the napkin over and tuck the lower left corner and the lower right corner into each other.

Use a napkin with a border or one with a design in one corner for the "spire" or the "double door." If a napkin has a design, make sure that it is at the lower corner as you start folding.

55a   Pull down both tips of the "spire."

55b   Pull down the center point.

56   Follow the instructions for the "spire," but tuck in the corners without turning the napkin over. See 54b.

56

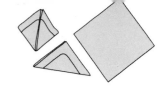

57   King's Robe
58   Lily

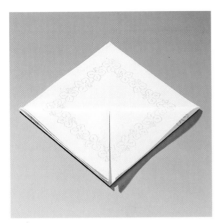

57a   After completing the three basic steps, fold both upper tips at the middle, and then fold them down.

57b   Fold down the tip of the upper triangle.

As a final elegant touch, use real lilies in the flower arrangement. The lily theme is repeated by the folded napkin.

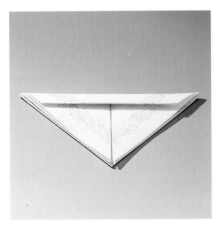

57c   Fold the upper portion down to the midline, and again at the midline to create a triangle.

57d   Tuck both outer corners into each other in the back, and then pull down the "train" of the "robe."

58   Tuck the tips of the "train" into the cuff.

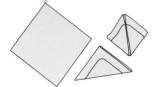

59 Swan

Use 20 × 20″ napkins for the "swan" design. The napkins must be very well starched and reinforced with extra-heavy aluminum foil to give the form its stability. Forming the neck requires a certain amount of effort.

59a After the initial basic steps, turn the napkin, and fold both sides to the middle.

59b Fold both halves together and with the open side pointing down, then form the neck.

59c Turn the napkin over, set it on the table and, while supporting the body, turn the neck up and the beak forward.

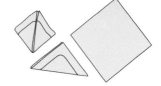

The swan (or peacock) design is often used as a centerpiece. For a centerpiece, use a very large napkin (32″ × 32″) or a large piece of fabric. The "pointed triple fan" or the "double-pointed triple fan" can be used for the "plumage." See folding instructions 30 and 31.

59d The "Chinese junk" or the "triple fan" can be used as "plumage." See folding instructions 31 and 35.

59e This is how the "plumage" is attached to the body.

60 Stand the triple fan upright to form the peacock.

Group C

1   Each design begins with the unfolded napkin, left ("wrong") side of the napkin facing up. The napkin must be perfectly square.

2   Fold both the left and the right corners to the middle, while supporting the material with your thumbnail in the middle of the upper edge.

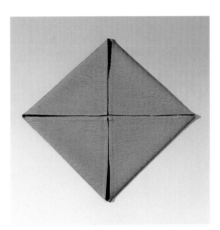

3   Fold the two lower corners as you did in step 2. Pay particular attention if some of the following instructions read: "Turn the napkin over," since the final outcome depends a great deal upon this step.

61 Angel Wing
62 Double Arch

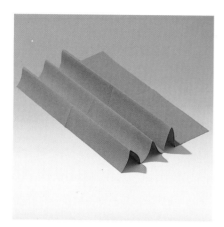

61a   Fold the napkin in six to eight equal folds.

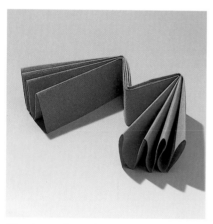

61b   Crease the napkin in the center, and then fold each side into "wings."

For these folds, and especially for the "double arch," the napkins should not be too big. Paper napkins are particularly good for these folds.

62a   Fold the napkin in six to eight equal folds. Fold the left end to the middle.

62b   Repeat on the other side. Reinforce both folds.

62c   Unfold both fans, as shown.

63 Folding Screen

63a Fold the napkin into four equal folds. Fold both ends quarter-way to the middle.

63b Turn the napkin over and then fold both ends to the middle.

63c Pull the ends up and towards the middle, as shown.

You could make *eight* initial folds. This will add to the napkin's elegance and it will make it more decorative.

64a   Position napkin with corners pointing up/down, left/right. Fold left and right corners to the middle, covering the foil.

64d   Fold the napkin together at its long axis and reinforce all of the creases.

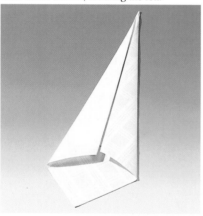

64b   Fold both sides to the middle; then fold the lower tip to the inside.

64e   Pull the neck up and the beak out.

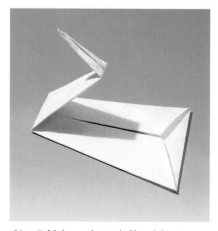

64c   Fold the napkin in half, and then turn the left tip back.

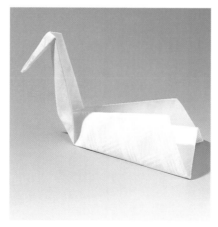

64f   Reinforce these folds again and then set the swan on the table, opening the napkin up.

This swan was folded from a 17″ × 17″ napkin. It would make a
wonderful decoration for a cold buffet table, or it could be the
centerpiece for a festive table setting.

65 Swaying Palm
66 Bouquet

65a   Fold a flat napkin exactly as shown in this photo.

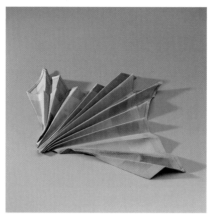

65b   Pleat the napkin, starting from the corner down to the middle of the midline.

66   Hold the napkin at the lower center; then turn it upside down and shake it out.

Both of these designs look best when inserted into a glass. A variation would be to tie the napkin together at the end with a ribbon, or to insert it partially into a napkin ring.

67 Asparagus
68 Rifle

67a   Fold the upper and the lower edges to the middle.

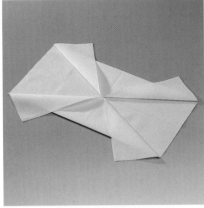

67b   Turn all four corners to the outside.

67c   Roll the napkin from both sides to the middle.

68a   To make the rifle, turn the asparagus form over.

68b   Fold the napkin together in the middle and then tuck the ends into each other.

Use the "rifle" design when game is served. Use the "asparagus" design when that vegetable is served. Use a light green napkin.

69 Double Fan
70 Pointed Double Fan

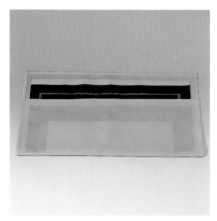

69a   Fold the lower edge of the napkin up to one-third below the upper edge. Insert a paper napkin in a contrasting color.

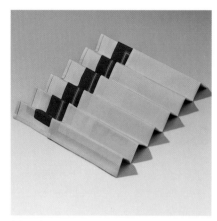

69b   Pleat the napkin into approximately 1″-wide folds.

70   For the "pointed double fan," pull out the points of the lower portion of the folds.

The contrasting color of the paper napkin is a wonderful way to emphasize the color scheme of the table setting.

71 Rosette

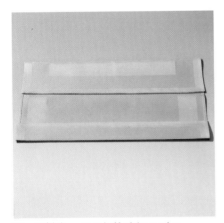

71a   Fold the upper half of the napkin down to the middle, and fold the lower half of the napkin quarter-way up to the middle.

71b   Fold the lower edge up, slightly above the middle.

The rosette shown here has six pleats, while the one shown on page 76 has only five. This gives a very different effect.

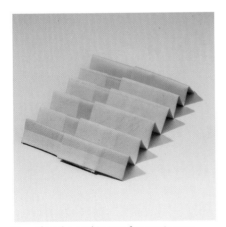

71c   Pleat the napkin into five or six even folds.

71d   Pull out the deep part of the lower portion of the napkin.

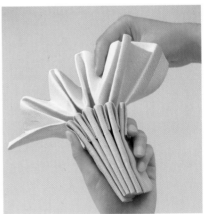

71e   Pull back the top portion of the folds and then reinforce the creases at that point.

72 Half-Moon
73 Full Moon

These moon-shaped napkins look particularly good on a royal blue tablecloth, sprinkled with star-shaped confetti. If you use a 20″ × 20″ napkin, the "full moon" will cover the whole dinner plate.

72a Pleat the napkin into six or eight folds.

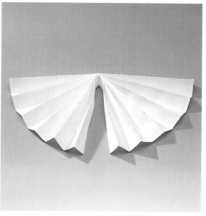

72b Hold the napkin in the middle and unfold the pleats.

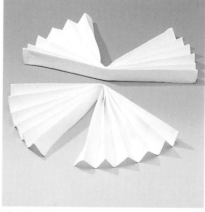

73 To make the "full moon," fold two "half-moons," and then attach them to each other.

74 Star

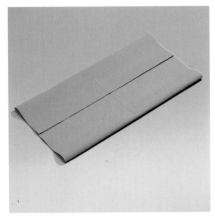

74a Fold the upper and the lower edges to the middle.

74b Fold the napkin together at the middle, and then reinforce the crease.

The "star" design is decorative and easy to make. It can be made from paper napkins, as well.

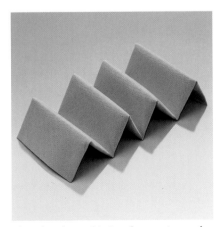

74c Pleat the napkin into four or six equal folds.

74d Hold the napkin firmly at the middle, and then pull out the tips of the pleats.

74e Turn the napkin around and repeat pulling out the rest of the pleats.

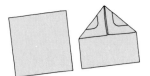

75 Sail

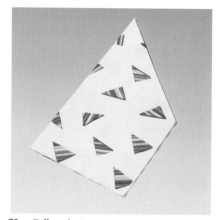

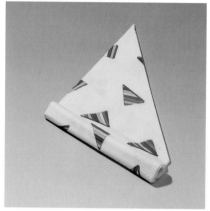

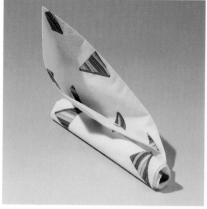

75a Follow the instructions for the first basic steps for Group C, and then fold the napkin in half vertically.

75b Roll the lower portion of the napkin up to the middle.

75c Stand the napkin upright and then open the triangle.

Crease the triangle (the sail) before rolling up the lower portion. This will keep the "sail" upright.

76 Fan with Corners

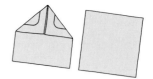

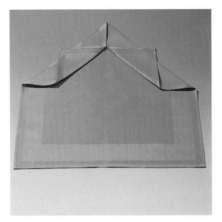

76a Follow the first two basic steps for Group C; then fold back both tips in the middle of the triangle.

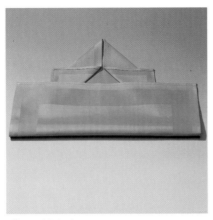

76b Fold the lower portion up so that the triangle is still visible.

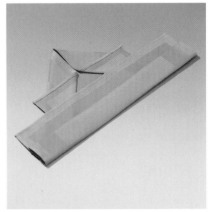

76c Fold the lower edge up so that you have three segments of equal size.

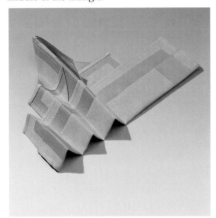

76d Starting from the middle, fold the left side into three equal pleats.

76e Repeat on the right side.

This is an easy folding method. This napkin fold is very decorative—insert it into a glass or place it flat on a plate.

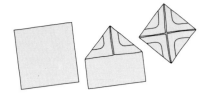

77 Lotus
78 Water Lily

77a Complete all three basic steps for Group C. Fold all four corners to the middle.

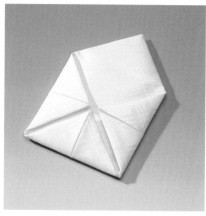

77b Turn the napkin over and again fold all four corners to the middle.

77c First pull out the tips that are underneath the four corners; then continue with the inside tips.

78a After completing the three basic steps for Group C, turn the napkin over and repeat folding all four corners to the middle.

79a Follow the instructions for the "lotus," but do not pull out the tips from underneath the four corners.

80a Fold the four corners of the "flower pillow" to the middle instead of lifting the tips up.

78b While holding the middle securely, carefully pull out the four corners.

74

79b Turn the napkin over, lift up all of the tips and then put a flower arrangement in the middle.

80b Turn the napkin over again and square the corners, and then fold them to the outside.

79 Flower Pillow
80 Cross

To make the four napkin designs on the opposite page, pay special attention to *when* you turn the napkin over.

After-Theatre Dinner

After an evening at the theatre, it is particularly nice to dine at a beautifully decorated table. Your guests, dressed in their best festive attire, will not be upstaged when the table decorations are done in delicate tones, like the blue-grey shown in this photo. The napkins are made of the same fabric as the tablecloth, and are folded into a rosette (see page 69).

The place cards have been decorated with tragic and comic masks. You could easily make them yourself.

The late hour of an after-theatre dinner requires that the menu consist of light fare.

Silver Anniversary

If you have decided to celebrate your silver anniversary in style, it is a good idea to turn the arrangements over to a capable caterer. There are always enough details left that still need your personal attention. Some of these details might include writing and sending the invitations, scheduling the events of the day, determining the menu, and arranging accommodations for overnight guests.

As with all other events, an early meeting with the caterer is very important to assure that all arrangements are done properly and that everything is well coordinated. A silver wedding anniversary calls for a festive but calm decorating theme. The choice of dinnerware, silverware, and stemware can all add to the theme. Menus and place cards, as well as other accessories, can be crafted in shades of silver, and the "25" can be incorporated in the centerpiece.

The couple has shared 25 good years. It is only fitting that this milestone be celebrated by family and friends. The setting pictured here consists of four courses: soup, a warm dish with white wine, a main course with red wine, and as a fitting conclusion, dessert and champagne.

Business Dinner

Here is an example of a dinner for journalists. It takes very little to adapt the idea to other types of businesses.

The tablecloth is real newspaper, covered with clear plastic. Add an old typewriter to establish the theme. The black and white of the newpaper is echoed with the use of black dinnerware and white napkins. The napkins are folded into an envelope (see page 46). If you don't like black dinnerware, use black place mats only.

Use magazine pages for the tablecloth instead of newspaper for an entirely different flavor.

Skipper

This table setting is meant to evoke the joy and the memories of a day at sea. Everything is in shades of beige and brown, the colors of the wood used to build the boat. The compass card must give the proper direction. Don't hesitate to add the compass to the table decoration.

The nautical atmosphere is enhanced by using wooden plates, and silverware with wooden handles. The ship in the bottle adds a very special touch. It is still possible to create a very nice table setting, even without these nautical touches.

Color-coordinated napkins are folded into "bouquets" (see page 66) and are inserted into one of the wine glasses.

Black Pearl

This is a table setting for a small dinner party for very special and important business associates. The red place mats contrast with the black tablecloth. The arrangement of the glassware is determined by the shape of the place mats. Golden flatware and the hint of a red-gold glow emphasize the elegant note of the event. Napkins, dyed black, decorated with a golden border and folded into a fan shape (see page 34) round out this harmonious picture.

The place cards, golden black to match the decoration of the table setting, are really menus, printed in three languages—German, French, and English.

Future 2000

This table setting offers a glimpse into the future. The color combination is a metallic grey-blue, reminiscent of the colors of outer space. The use of mirrors and iridescent glass marbles creates a shimmering, unreal light when properly illuminated. Not only will the dinnerware, the silverware, and the napkins (rolled into obelisks) attract attention, but the combination of light-reflecting, shimmering objects will cause a sensation.

Japanese Theme

While red is the traditional Japanese color, we chose a variation in salmon pink. The delicate tablecloth sets the tone. The Japanese theme is emphasized by the dinnerware, with a black accent, and by the choice of pink flowers. The menus imitate Japanese screens, adding to the unusual setting. A candle behind each menu gives the image of a Japanese house with its windows illuminated. Black napkins with salmon-colored paper inserts complete the picture. The napkins are the "maid's cap" (page 26), and the "bishop's hat" (page 54).

The choice of appropriate flowers as well as the wreath underscore the unusual Japanese flavor of this table setting.

Gala Dinner

Weddings, receptions, important conferences: these are some reasons to give a gala dinner. Such an affair requires a great deal of expertise on the part of the chef, and a great deal of organizational talent on the part of the caterer and his staff who will decorate the hall and set the table.

Serve an appetizer after the aperitif. Any food decoration and garnish for a gala dinner is done in the kitchen prior to serving. This is the job of the caterer and the waiter/waitress. Serving hot food under a cloche (dome) adds a special touch to the meal. Serve a liqueur or brandy with mocha or espresso as a fitting conclusion to a gala meal.

The menu begins with soup. The rounded, smaller spoon tells us that the soup will be served in a cup. The next course is a hot hors d'oeuvre accompanied by a white wine. The fish dish is served with a second white wine. The main course is served with a red wine. The silverware for dessert tells us that dessert will be sweet and that it will be accompanied by champagne.

Testimonial

A testimonial dinner can be arranged in many different ways. Perhaps you have invited your business associates to celebrate the success of a particular venture or to honor the "man (or woman) of the hour." The table setting should then be somewhat neutral, while the menu might elaborate on the theme. A short reception (something to make your friends unwind and feel relaxed) might precede the dinner.

This photo (opposite page) shows how to decorate a table to celebrate the successful conclusion of a student's advanced course in carpentry. The student's colleagues have organized the dinner to honor the graduate. The decoration expresses the theme by using wood shavings and similar items.

The caterer must know the host's wishes to be able to decorate the table. The host is responsible for creating a good impression and a congenial atmosphere. It is important that the caterer and the host discuss all the details in advance. The choice of serving either a full-course meal or simply a buffet is wholly at the discretion of the host, and depends on the number of guests, and on the atmosphere the host wants to create.

The party's theme is emphasized by the use of the wood shavings wrapped around the menu, and by the plane that serves as the centerpiece. The table setting tells us that the menu consists of a cold fish appetizer served with white wine, followed by soup, and then by a main course, served with red wine. Dessert will conclude the affair.

Dinner for Two

Caterers usually only arrange large parties. Arranging a "dinner for two" is rather the exception. A caterer could adopt this idea as an option he offers to the public. It is also a wonderful chance to fulfill a client's special wishes.

You could probably find many reasons for having a "dinner for two": to celebrate a personal or private anniversary, a graduation or a birthday. You might recreate a very special event the two of you enjoyed in the past, perhaps recreating the menu of that event. One of you might want to plan a surprise. In that case, the caterer needs to know all the details—the atmosphere, the menu, and the table decoration—in order to make the evening a success.

Silverware (from left to right): gourmet spoon, oyster fork, lobster fork, caviar knife and caviar spoon.

Two people can celebrate all by themselves—there's no need to wait for a special occasion. This table is set for two to enjoy a few special candle-lit hours with caviar and champagne.

Index